DISCOVERING THE AMERICAN STORK

DISCOVERING

Words by Jack Denton Scott

Photographs by Ozzie Sweet

THE AMERICAN STORK

HARCOURT   BRACE   JOVANOVICH

NEW YORK AND LONDON

Printed in the United States of America

First edition

B   C   D   E   F   G   H   I   J   K

Library of Congress Cataloging in Publication Data

Scott, Jack Denton, 1915-
Discovering the American stork.

SUMMARY: Describes the habits and habitats of the
American stork and the efforts of conservationists to
save this unusual bird.
    1. Wood stork—Juvenile literature.   2. Birds—
North America—Juvenile literature.   [1. Wood stork.
2. Storks]   I. Sweet, Ozzie.   II. Title.
QL696.C535S4   598.3'4   75-41393
ISBN 0-15-203055-7

The stilt-legged, sword-billed, storied stork is one of the world's most spectacular birds. But what do most of us actually know about the stork? The folktale that it brings babies, lives only in Holland, and nests on chimneys of Dutch homes?

That the stork family is so large that it includes three tribes, six genera, and seventeen species will come as a surprise to many. The fact that America in recent years has discovered one of its most colorful and spectacular birds to be living incognito, passing as a species that it isn't, has startled even the ornithologists. America has a stork!

In contrast to our bird of mystery, the sixteen other species have the names that physically describe them clearly spelled out, or they bear exotic-sounding names that excite the imagination. Ranging throughout Europe, Africa, the Middle and Far East, Australia, and South America are Abdim's stork (the smallest, the size of a chicken), the adjutants (greater and lesser), the African openbill, the Asian openbill, the black and black-necked, the jabiru, the maguari, the marabou (the ugliest, looking like a vulture, with a favorite diet of young crocodiles), the milky stork, the painted, the saddlebill, the white, the woolly-necked, and the yellow-billed.

All are exceptional birds, some, such as the white stork, standing half as tall as a man; the largest, the jabiru, is man-sized. Besides their stalklike legs and abnormally long bills, they have colorful plumage, running from pink and pearl gray to stunning combinations of jet black and snowy white, and a stately appearance, both in the air and on the ground.

Partly because storks are so physically striking, they have become the subjects of many legends since ancient times. For Americans, the most famous is the white stork, probably because during the summer months it inhabits continental Europe, the place where many of us came from and where much of our culture originated. This large white bird with black wing feathers, red bill, and red legs is the one most of us know as the stork through literature, folk art, photographs, and our travels to Europe, where they are landmark sights in many villages. Most countries in Europe (not England, where the stork was introduced but wouldn't stay) are proud of their housetop population of white storks.

Because this stork chose to live close to man, nesting during the summer on the highest rooftops, and was closely observed, many folktales and beliefs have originated—some farfetched, most humorous, many even weird.

Some Scandinavian, German, and Dutch parents still tell their children that babies are brought by the stork. They also say that the stork bit the mother's leg when bringing the baby, causing her to stay in bed for a while.

In Germany even today, it is believed that a stork flying over a house means that there will be a birth there and that its nesting on a house is a sign of good fortune. Wagon wheels and shallow baskets are placed on roofs and church clock towers to entice the good-luck birds to nest.

Noting that storks often visited swamps, marshes, and ponds, ancient belief had it that it was in these places that the souls of unborn children lived and there that the storks picked up infants and flew them to their rightful homes.

For centuries, all over Europe people watched the storks, working in teams, skillfully building their nests and returning to them each year. The birds' care of their young created tales of faithfulness in marriage and home life and eventually brought about the legend of their bringing babies, and using the stork's likeness on birth announcements.

The Scandinavians also have a folktale that claims the stork once had a voice and flew over Christ on the cross crying, "*Styrke! Styrke!*" ("Strength! Strength!")

Old Germanic tribes considered the stork sacred and severely punished anyone molesting the bird.

But high regard for the stork dates back even further, to 330 B.C., when Aristotle wrote that in northern Greece it was a crime to kill a stork. It was believed that the bird protected homes from lightning and evil spirits.

The Romans respected the stork's protectiveness toward its family so much that they passed the famous "Stork's Law," *Lex Ciconaria*, which compelled children to take care of their needy parents during their old age. This grew out of early observations of the stork's concern and attention toward both its young and old. Legends developed telling how young storks cared for the aged, weak, and sometimes blind parents, of how they carried these incapacitated birds around on their wings and carefully fed them.

Even the stork's name contributed to the legend, coming originally from the ancient Greek word *storgé*, meaning an innate natural affection. In the sacred language of the Hebrews the stork is described as "the pious one."

The long-legged bird was also assumed to possess certain powers. As early as Pliny, it was believed that drunkenness could be cured by eating storks' eggs. From the earliest times it was considered bad luck to kill a stork, and many people believed that storks once were men.

There were some legend makers and storytellers who disagreed on the beneficial power of storks. In Morocco, it was thought that if a stork built its nest on a roof, the house would become empty; if in trees, the trees would wither. They believed that if storks were clean and white when they arrived, there would be much sunshine and warm weather, but if they were dirty, it would be a bad year.

In the Middle East, people believed that when storks left their rooftop nests and built other nests in trees, it was a certain sign of war. If they abandoned their nests, great calamity was sure to befall the area. It has also been factually recorded that storks have departed en masse from a region before a pestilence struck.

In Europe, the stork's disappearance in winter was a mystery embroidered with fantasy. During medieval days nothing was known about the migration of birds, so one belief had the storks flying to Egypt in winter and changing into men. Having been men part of the time, it was natural for the birds to want to live close to their own kind, on their rooftops, when they returned for the summer months.

The unnamed editor in Volume VI of *The Harleian Miscellany* (1744–1746) wrote that the stork flew to the moon to spend the winter months. "It has to be fact," the author stated, "because of the length of time the stork is absent from its summer nesting place. Two months are occupied in upward flight, three months for rest and replenishment on the moon, and two months for the return passage."

In reality, the white stork does have a long way to migrate from Europe to Africa, departing by two routes. From Holland, Spain, and the Rhine Valley, the storks fly across the Strait of Gibraltar. Flying so high on the Spanish side that they are mere specks in the sky, they then glide across the open water to North Africa.

Those storks east of the Elbe River go by a southeasterly route, crossing the Dardanelles and the Bosporus, flying along the eastern shore of the Mediterranean, flapping across Turkey, Syria, Lebanon, and Israel, then on into Egypt. Flocks merge, until one flight can contain thousands of birds. They follow the Nile River in Egypt southward, across the Great Rift Valley of Kenya and Tanganyika to South Africa.

For Danish storks it may *seem* like a flight to the moon, more than eight thousand miles.

On that long migration the storks conserve energy by soaring and ascending on thermals (rising columns of warm air), thus gaining enough altitude to glide to the next thermal. This works well over land, but across the sea good thermals are scarce, so the storks must use their wings. This not only is tiring but also sometimes fatal, as often there are storms and strong winds.

Danger appears in other ways too. One year a violent hailstorm in South Africa killed 172 migrating storks. Dry spells also take their toll. During one crossing of the Sahara Desert in August, two thousand storks died. At an oasis Arabs killed five hundred grounded storks that were already half dead from thirst. The desert people thought the birds were gifts from heaven to compensate for the loss of their date crop.

Today, in Europe and elsewhere, the white stork is vanishing. In addition to migration dangers, drained marshes reducing food supply, roofs of modern buildings offering few nesting sites, television antennas, high-tension wires, and telephone lines presenting flying hazards, many storks are being killed by DDT. Recent reports place the population in the mere hundreds.

In comparison, our stork, hiding incognito for so long, has been doing well. Concerned people and a remote location helped. But the bird did have serious troubles with the complications created by civilization and was nearly wiped out. How and why it is now beginning to flourish is the foundation of this story and the bird's own modern legend.

Explanations are fuzzy as to why the American stork was called the wood ibis by birdmen, and there is no sound reasoning for books still referring to it by that name. Not only is *Mycteria americana,* the American wood stork, not an ibis (it isn't even in the same family of birds as the white ibis and the glossy ibis), it is the only true stork found in North America.

Wood storks rank high in the species clan Ciconiidae. The three others, the yellow-billed, the painted (not only the prettiest, but at five feet the tallest of the four wood storks), and the milky stork—respectively from Africa, India, and Indochina—along with our wood stork possess distinct personalities that set them apart from other storks. For example, their striking preening displays and balancing and gaping acts during mating are common to wood storks.

A true aristocrat of the large stork family, our brown-eyed stork is large, about the size of a Canada goose, with a length up to forty-eight inches and weighing between six and eleven pounds. The stilt legs are grayish blue, the webbed feet tinged yellow. Plumage is pure white, and the flight feathers are ebony, the black and white in vivid contrast. The tail is very short, greenish black, tinged with purple. The blue-gray head is featherless, and the dark gray nine-inch bill, thick at the base, has a dramatic down curve like a cutlass. Aloft, the stork has a five-and-a-half-foot wingspan, flies with neck and legs stretched straight out, and looks like no other bird in America. Once seen, the wood stork is not forgotten. Sexes are look-alikes, with the female somewhat smaller than the male. In fact, they are so much alike that sometimes there is confusion at mating time.

In southwestern Florida, there once was a dramatic wilderness where great bald cypress trees, twenty-five feet in girth and as tall as ten-story buildings, marched like an army of giants into the misty Everglades beyond. This area was known as Big Cypress.

No more. The big trees are gone, with mainly the much smaller pond cypress left. These trees, unlike their great cousins, lose their foliage in winter; thus what used to be a permanent leafy wilderness now in winter appears to be a forest of stunted dead trees shrouded in wind-spun gray moss.

What had happened was termed progress, which comes in many guises; in this case it was the slaughter of the big cypresses to obtain lumber. In the early 1930s, eight sawmills moved into the Big Cypress area, and by 1956 most of the trees had been felled.

Many of the trees were cut down even while storks were nesting in their tops. Little was known of them in those days. As far back as could be recalled, these long-legged, long-billed birds had been there as long as the trees, which had been growing in this swampland for seven centuries. Florida names for our stork ranged from gourdhead, gannet, ironhead, and flinthead to preacher, the last sobriquet given them because of their sober, dignified mien.

Mycteria americana

The strange birds did not have the showy nuptial plumes and fancily curled feathers of some of the other wading species such as egrets, so hunters had not killed them for their plumage. They weren't a gamebird, and their flesh wasn't palatable. Thus, the storks, which no one knew were storks, had a built-in protection in man's lack of interest—until men moved in and began destroying their nesting habitat.

In addition, farther south much construction was taking place near Lake Okeechobee, draining the Everglades and dropping the water level. Fires occurred often, destroying the organic soil and thus further reducing the water-holding capacity of the Everglades. At first this didn't affect the storks too much. They simply flew to mangroves deeper in the swampland. But during the periods of severe drought, all the freshwater marshes that held the fish which were the wood storks' mainstay were pathetic puddles of mud. Many of the birds starved.

Before this onslaught of drought, drainage, and lumbering, it was believed that there were about thirty thousand storks in the Big Cypress area, fifty thousand in the region that is now Everglades National Park, and several smaller colonies throughout the rest of the state, bringing the total to over a hundred thousand.

An egret

By 1954, birdmen, using aerial surveys, made an expert guess that the population was down to less than eight thousand. These same conservationists, who were beginning to recognize the stork for what it was, formed a group and sought the help of the National Audubon Society to find a preserve for the fast-disappearing birds.

They had noticed the storks flying over an area deep in the swampland in the northwest corner of what used to be Big Cypress. A stream of water, Corkscrew Creek, snaked into a dense, unknown region called Corkscrew Swamp, encompassing only about three miles of an original untouched wild strand twenty miles long. This also was about to be invaded by the lumber companies, for here grew the largest remaining giant bald cypresses in North America. Here, too, although it wasn't known then, was the last large concentration of wood storks in the United States.

The Audubon Society appealed to the various interests that owned or leased Corkscrew Swamp and suggested the formation of a sanctuary. Through the generosity of individuals and the

Lee Tidewater Cypress Company and the Collier Company, in 1954 that suggestion became reality, and the National Audubon Society's Corkscrew Swamp Sanctuary was born, with 6,000 acres under the society's protection and control. Later, gifts and acquisitions increased the sanctuary to 10,880 acres.

So not only were the last of the great bald cypresses saved, along with the stork population of what then was estimated at about four thousand pairs, but a pristine wilderness was also preserved, the likes of which is becoming most rare in America.

This sanctuary could be the last breeding place in America that offers the ideal food, protection, and seclusion that wood storks need.

Small breeding colonies once existed in South Carolina, Georgia, and Louisiana, but now nesting in the United States, as far as experts can determine, occurs only in Florida. The storks' range outside of North America is not well known, but some nesting has been observed in Central and South America.

Although the birds are seen in central Florida, the Everglades National Park, Pelican Island, and a few other places in Florida, the world's largest wood-stork nesting colony is in the Corkscrew Swamp Sanctuary. Records have been kept there since its inception, which show that in a peak nesting season (such as 1960–1961) six thousand pairs of storks produced seventeen thousand young. After that there was a decline, with less successful results, until the 1970–1971 season, when the upswing began again and is continuing.

As it involves reproduction of the species, the nesting activity is the most important of all. Even in this, wood storks are different. Most birds in America begin to breed in the spring as the days lengthen. Not wood storks. They watch water levels. When the water in ponds, marshes, and streams falls, schools of fish are concentrated in pools, making them easier to catch. Wood storks then time their breeding so the young can be raised when fish are plentiful and accessible.

Despite such timing, nesting failures can result from exceptionally heavy rainfall, dry spells, and drainage and development in the vicinity of Corkscrew Swamp, reducing, and in some cases eliminating, feeding areas.

But the storks in Corkscrew Swamp Sanctuary are lucky, since the National Audubon Society is establishing the world's first major experiment in managed food production for them and other wading birds on acquired land adjoining Corkscrew Swamp. The society has created a fish farm, which will help during times of drought and excessive rainfall. Eleven ponds have been built on twenty-six acres and stocked with "rough" fish—gambusia, shiners, sunfish, and other species that the storks like. There is a trough running through the center of each pond in which the level of the water can be lowered so that the storks can easily grasp the fish with their bills.

But a shortage of fish caused by abnormal weather may be the lesser enemy. The big threat lurks outside the sanctuary; in fact, has it surrounded. The land developers are all around Corkscrew Swamp Sanctuary, impatient to get in and drain it, fell the old giant cypresses, drive out the storks, and erect condominiums. Collier County, in which the storks are making their last stand, has been overrun by dubious progress that has converted lovely countryside into concrete ugliness, and local politicians eye Corkscrew Swamp skeptically, still to be convinced that the place is for the birds.

The National Audubon Society claims it not only is a sanctuary for birds but also for men seeking the healing balm of quiet places and wildlife. Shortly after Audubon acquired it, they built a sturdy elevated boardwalk over the black ooze of the swamp, where no man could walk and no boat push its prow through the tangle of water plants and invisible underwater roots. The boardwalk runs from pine flatwoods at the eastern edge across saw grass and swales of "wet prairie" through the stand of pond cypress that rings Corkscrew Swamp.

The "wet prairie" of Corkscrew Swamp

As visitors move across the boardwalk through the gloom of the moss-hung pond cypresses, they suddenly emerge into a wild wonderland undisturbed for centuries. The silence is broken only by mysterious splashings in the plant-spangled water and by the occasional sleepy hoot of an owl and the trills and warblings of unidentified birds hidden in the leafy wild beyond, their sounds like a symphony orchestra tuning up. "Lettuce lakes," mirror-still ponds, are afloat with emerald foliage; ferns the color of rare Chinese jade stand like sculpture, lacy, metal-perfect in design; orchids burst from tree trunks in explosions of breathtaking beauty; swamp ash, strangler fig, trees and plants that only the experts can identify abound. This is nature's hothouse with such a riotous growth of rare plant life that botanists come from many miles to view it.

This is a "climax" forest that has never been disturbed, a

completely natural world where a variety of wildlife survives secure in its freedom and invisible protection. It makes the "captive" world of the zoo pale in comparison. Not bold, but visible, are fox squirrels, raccoons, bears, otters, alligators, snakes, lizards that look like animated jewelry, turtles great and small. Herons blue as a summer sky, dignified brown pelicans, white ibis in flight like a flurry of snowflakes, egrets, anhingas, cormorants, and roseate spoonbills flash, spin, and glide in this aviary watched by sentinels that stand with their heads in the sky, the awesomely high bald cypresses that are also making their last stand here in the inner forest of Corkscrew Swamp Sanctuary.

Higher even than the rare giants, the wood storks stretch their wings five feet and more in a silent soar above the trees or glissade in controlled slides across the sky.

Occasionally three or more storks will vie for the same limb perch, fluttering in their own graceful ballet dance, or a stork and a brown pelican will almost touch beaks as they skim over the swamp. This friend of the stork, the brown pelican, is an endangered species (although it is making a comeback in Florida). The pesticides DDT and DDE are concentrated in the pelicans' bodies as a result of their eating fish from chemically polluted waters. This often produces eggshells too thin to support the weight of the adult nesting pelicans. Remarkably, even though it also eats fish, the wood stork does not yet seem to be affected.

Vying for a perch

In this swampland show, there is no doubt that the stork is the main performer. It is everywhere, standing in the shallows of a lettuce lake, its tall legs propping it up so that it looks supported from above; on patches of dry land, where it moves in a slow, dignified, erect walk; on limbs of cypress or mangroves, where it stands like a somber judge in black-and-white robes, peering through the filigree of Spanish moss as if pondering a difficult decision.

Nearly every bald cypress is festooned with stork nests. Although wood storks do not live near men as the white storks do, preferring the deep, remote solitude of this swampland where time has stood still, the human visitors who have been coming here since 1955 do not disturb them.

A female stork watches

a male select a nesting site . . .

The storks may stand and stare back, or they may seem oblivious, even mating while under observation. That act can begin with the female balancing on a limb as skillfully as a circus tightrope walker. The mating behavior of wood storks is dramatically different from that of most birds.

The male finds the nest site, then perches or sits there, aggressively driving off other storks, both male and female. The place he has selected to make his stand as a somewhat peculiar suitor at the beginning of the mating season, which may start in November or December or even as late as May, could be a nest he had used the year before or the site where he wishes to establish a new nest. Or, if he is three years old, he may be making his first attempt at mating.

. . . then tries her luck.

The behavior of other males is unpredictable. They may get the message, when the stork at the nest site rears up clacking its bill, and bypass that tree, or they may challenge and attack, either taking over that territory or being driven off. Fights can be extremely fierce, but no deaths have been recorded as the result of these duels with the long, sharp, horny bills. Visitors to Corkscrew Swamp Sanctuary stand fascinated at the swordplay, the birds dancing about as nimbly as fencers.

A female in the mating mood moves in on the male at the nest tree, testing him. He doesn't respond to the approaching female, fiercely driving her off. She flees, but soon returns, making another approach. Again with a furious flurry of wings he pecks her away. If she is really interested and ready to mate, she will come back a third time. Sometimes the male will again drive her away, but if she is stubborn and continues her approach, each attack becomes less fierce until finally the female stands beside the male.

While these approaches and attacks at the nest are under way, both male and female make unusual ritualistic social displays, which are really signals sent to reduce aggression.

Feathers play a large part in these displays—and a great deal more; without them the bird could not survive. Without feathers the stork not only couldn't fly, but would die in extremes of temperatures, for feathers are great insulators. And, as extensions of tail and wings, they are flight surfaces, composites containing feathers within feathers. The quill of the feather has two rows of barbs, which together form the "vane." Each of these two barbs has two more rows of smaller barbs, "barbules," and these in turn have another tiny fringe of curved hooks growing out of them called "barbicels." These are clustered so tightly that air cannot be forced through the feather. Thus, when the wings are pressed down, flight results from this accumulated resistance that the flight feathers make to the air, enabling the bird at every oaring of a wing to stroke a wingful of air downward.

In flight, the wingspan reaches a width of 5½ feet.

Thus birds must keep their feathers in good condition. To do this, they engage in various grooming acts: preening, scratching, feather settling, bathing, bill wiping.

At the approach of a female during the mating season, male wood storks preen their feathers or pretend to strip down the feathers of a partially open wing. Often the bill doing the preening doesn't even touch the feather. Birds at nest sites in Corkscrew Swamp Sanctuary can be seen in this machine-like motion for several minutes at a time, the male often moving its bill from one wing to the other.

This preening behavior indicates to the female that the male, although he may appear to be aggressive, is really interested in finding a mate. To signal that she is too, she goes into a "balancing posture," walking along a limb as close as she can get to the male, spreading her wings and agilely balancing on the limb. As she does this, she opens her bill wide in a "gaping display," then spreads her wings briefly, but continues gaping. She keeps her bill open even when the male permits her to stand beside him.

These displays are important to wood storks, bird experts believing that, because the sexes look alike, this attack-and-retreat, preening, and gaping routine may be the only method storks have of telling male from female.

After the storks become a pair, they engage in another display, called "up-down," when one bird comes back to the nest or nest site after a brief absence. As the returning bird alights, both throw their heads upward in an extreme position until the bill is vertical. Then they open the bills and gape, lower their heads and hiss, then slowly swing their heads from side to side.

In the breeding act the male, atop the female, clatters his mandibles (upper and lower beaks) together and clicks his bill against hers while both spread their wings.

Building the nest is a team effort. The female stays at the site while the male makes many trips searching for sticks. He

It takes about three days to build the nest.

brings them back, and the pair build the nest together, sometimes at a height of more than a hundred feet. The bald cypress
trees become apartment dwellings, some trees holding as many as
twenty nests. Storks appear to be good neighbors, staying strictly
to their own territory on branches near the nest, which is between two and three feet in diameter. It takes the pair about
three days to build the rather flimsy stick nest.

Usually on the fifth day after the pair is joined, the first
dull white egg is laid and is immediately incubated. Other eggs
are laid at intervals of one to two days until there is a clutch of
two to five eggs. The stork pair share incubating duties, which
takes about one month. One of the birds remains on the eggs
during the entire period. The incubating bird may sit unmov-
ing for hours, or it may briefly rise to preen, exercise wings and
legs, turn the eggs with its bill, or even repair the nest.

When one stork returns to take over its duty on the eggs,
there is another display: the bird on the nest lifts itself off the
eggs, gapes, and from its open mouth comes a fizzing sound like
that from a newly opened bottle of champagne. Adult storks
make few other vocal sounds, occasionally a croak or a humming,
and apparently use various bill clackings to communicate.

Even in the laying of eggs, the storks seem to time it so
that, despite the food situation, some young will survive. After
a month, the adults do not sit on the eggs but stand and stare at
them, and this action, observers claim, is a sure sign that the eggs
are beginning to hatch. As the eggs were laid at intervals of one
to two days, the hatching takes place over a period of five days.
Thus the young are born varying in ages. If there is a plentiful
supply of food, all will survive. But if drought or other factors
reduce that supply, the smallest, last born, hatchlings will not.
This may seem a cruel law of nature, but it does ensure that the
fittest will live, rather than have insufficient food distributed to
all the nestlings and thus have all perish.

A parent's-eye view of the hatching would show a slow,

A parent's-eye view . . .

. . . of the hatching.

The newborn storks

laborious breaking of the egg barrier. The shell is tough, and even with the sharp egg tooth with which it is born, the hatchling takes a long time to crack and wiggle its way not only out of the eggshell but also out of the membrane that encases its body. When all the young storks are born, they lay huddled together, ugly, almost reptilian-looking, naked and helpless in the nest.

Unlike the lucky precocial species (ducks, geese, and trumpeter swans), which leave the nest almost as soon as they are out of the shell, wood storks are altricial, the young remaining in the nest until fully feathered and about ready to fly.

Although the newborn storks appear to be completely naked, if they could be closely examined, tiny tufts of down would be seen speckling their bodies. Later these tufts are pushed out by the second growth, which will become the true plumage. The almost invisible indication of the feathers to come

Sheltering the babies from the wind . . .

are dots, hundreds of them. Through these dots or pimples on
the skin, feathers will eventually emerge, quill, vane, barbs, and
all. But first the dots will become white, fluffy down, which is
then pushed out of its socket by a cellular mass beneath it. Those
cells continue to grow, lifting the down clear of the skin and
brushing it off like snow. Thus, in stages, the baby down is shed
in tatters and replaced by the true feathers, which overlap one
another like tiles on a roof.

But since the down does not grow for ten days, the baby
storks must be constantly attended by the parents. This involves
not only feeding but also brooding them for the first week. Even
though brooding may not continue after that period, except during rainy or cool weather, the parents stand over them and
shelter them from the wind and harmful rays of the sun. And
the wood storks may be the only birds that give their young
shower baths during hot weather. The parents fly to cool pools
and drink deeply, then return to the nest and stand over their
offspring, spraying them with water.

. . . with her lovely cape of feathers

(Leading stork expert Dr. M. Philip Kahl, Jr., discovered a method adult storks have for cooling themselves that also may be unique in the bird world. He found that at certain times in the summer, when, high in their treetop nests, they are exposed to extremely hot temperatures, the storks often excrete on their legs. Dr. Kahl has proved in experiments that the action is part of a thermo-regulatory mechanism acting to prevent hyperthermia by means of evaporative cooling of the blood supply to the legs and feet.)

Unfortunately, despite the storks' noted skill in feeding and caring for themselves and their young, their world also curiously contains juvenile delinquency. The parents of very young birds must be constantly alert for marauding bands of immature, unmated storks that wander the colony, often attacking nests, trying to drive off the parents. If successful, they destroy the eggs and the young.

Parent birds bravely try to beat off the attackers, but if they fail and the eggs or chicks are destroyed, within a week the pair will lay a second clutch and resume the normal breeding pattern. That cycle means an almost continuous round of feeding fledglings.

Like their parents, the young in the nest also engage in "gaping displays," opening their bills wide when they see their parents and uttering a muted scream that grows deeper and disappears as they mature. After the adult birds alight on the nest and regurgitate the food they have brought, which the nestlings eagerly gobble, the nest noise subsides until the birds are hungry again. But as hunger seems almost constant, stork nests are noisy ones.

A probable victim of juvenile delinquency

Fledged in woolly white down, front half of heads bare, with yellow bills, the young at three weeks are about half the size of their parents. They remain in the nest for fifty days, at which time the family has consumed around 440 pounds of food and the young birds can make short flights.

*Passing the time
of day*

Almost ready to leave the nest . . .

At about fifty-five days they are fully feathered and trying their wings, jumping up and down in the nest, flapping, taking turns in the exercise. They fly a few feet at first, extending the distance as they gain confidence. Corkscrew Swamp is aflutter with these awkward flyers that flap from tree to tree, with many parents watching from a daytime roosting tree, preening their feathers or standing on one leg with heads drawn into the shoulders as they observe the learning antics of their offspring.

. . . but never far from their parents' eyes

But even after they can fly about the colony, until they are seventy-five days old the young storks return to the nest to be fed and to roost near their parents at night. Often young in this stage can be seen following their mothers and fathers around the colony, gaping and grunting, begging to be fed. But the adults will feed them only at the nest.

*Parents must work hard
to keep their young in food.*

Feeding can involve as many as twelve meals a day. When newly hatched, the chicks are fed small amounts often. As they grow, so do the amounts, but the number of feedings then drops to three or four a day. A young stork is estimated to eat 500 four- to six-inch fish while it is in the nest.

During this development, the parents work hard to keep their young in food. A flight of twenty miles is common and as far as forty miles not unusual. The young are fed a variety of food—frogs, small reptiles, crustaceans, mollusks—but the main

diet is fish, fish that man does not use, warmouth, mosquitofish, sailfin mollie, flagfish, and other species of rough fish.

Fishing techniques are unique. Like all birds, the stork depends on its bill to provide it with food, but unlike most other birds, it uses that long, curved appendage in conjunction with its stiltlike legs and sensitive feet that skillfully serve the stork in securing its specialized diet. The tall legs take it through water, the feet act as a sort of radar, and the bill finds and grabs the food the feet helped locate. But the bill actually does most of the work and may be as sensitive as the feet.

The feet act as a sort of radar.

Commenting on the marvels of a bird's bill in *The Bird, Its Form and Function*, naturalist William Beebe wrote, "Tie a

man's hands and arms tightly behind his back, stand him on his
feet, and tell him that he must hereafter find and prepare his

food, build his house, defend himself from his enemies and perform all of the business of life in such a position, and what a pitiable object he would present! Yet this is not unlike what

Accompanied by two pelicans, a group of storks leaves for other fishing waters.

birds have to do. Almost every form of vegetable and animal life is used as food by one or another of the species of birds.

They have most intricately built homes; their methods of defense are to be numbered by the score; the care of their delicate plumage alone would seem to necessitate many and varied instruments; yet all this is made possible, and chiefly executed, by one small portion of the bird—its bill or beak."

That nine-inch-long and seven-inch-in-circumference-at-the-base bill isn't all that small a portion of the stork. And despite its clumsy appearance, it is used as versatilely as any other bird's, as weapon, as hand, as a means of communication, but its main function is in finding the highly specialized food that permits the species to survive. Storks prefer to hunt in low, wet country where vast swamps alternate with marshy meadows. Here they fish on the flats and in shallow pools left when the tide is out. If fish are scarce in these ideal areas, the storks' broad wings take them coasting silently over other likely places, sometimes many miles from their nesting trees. As it is with other characteristics of the stork, that flight is far from ordinary.

Although the bird seems ungainly on the ground with its long legs, heavy bill, and short tail, it is anything but clumsy aloft. Those tall, slender legs that look as fragile as flower stalks are actually powerful springs that push the stork into the air or take it across the ground in a high-stepping, stalking gait, seventy long steps a minute. When it takes off on a flight from the ground, the stately walk becomes a running jump, or sometimes several running jumps, the wings in rapid motion as it lifts off. From a perch, the takeoff posture is a low bend, then its strong legs propel the stork into the air, wings flapping fast, legs trailing downward; in seconds it is spinning away in the sky, the beat of its powerful wings soon taking it out of sight.

A low bend . . .

. . . then strong legs
  propel it into
    the air.

Aloft

Once aloft, the stork, master of thermals that it is, uses the rising warm air so adroitly that it can soar for long periods without flapping a wing. Often storks fly for fun, a flock putting on a spiraling performance that the pilot of a sailplane would envy. They catch the upsurging currents of air and rise with the updraft, higher and higher, soaring in graceful circles until they are mere dots in the atmosphere.

When descending, they often make steep dives at full speed, sometimes flipping over and over from side to side. Sometimes they come down slowly, drifting like parachutes, wings cupped, legs dangling straight down. In this type of descent the birds sometimes approach the landing tree at an angle of sixty degrees, but moving very slowly.

If they fly in the early morning before the thermals are abundant, they flap along, alternating the wing beats with short periods of sailing, with the wings held motionless. They have been timed up to thirty-three miles an hour when in flapping flight, flying at two hundred feet.

Descending

But generally, storks coast to their feeding grounds, letting the thermals do the work for them. They flap to a height where they find thermals are strongest, then set their wings and spiral upward. Their light bodies with extremely high buoyancy and slotted wing tips help them soar like windblown paper. When they reach the top of the thermal current at about two thousand feet, they peel off and glide to their fishing grounds, often gliding as far as fifteen miles without stirring a wing, arriving fresh without any energy expended. They also seem to be masters of timing, scheduling their return flight before the thermals die in late afternoon. But if they have overfished and stayed too late (which seldom happens) and they can't use those warm air currents to return to their homes, they often remain in the feeding areas overnight.

So, although they may sometimes glide and soar for pleasure, their flights are mainly all business, taking them to their fishing pools, where they always fish in groups. Fishing is accomplished by the tactile sense rather than by sight. In water usually not over fifteen inches deep, the storks wade gingerly, feeling for fish with their sensitive feet and long bills, perfect instruments for finding fish in turgid water that often is dense with vegetation.

The birds place their partially opened bills into the murky water, moving them slowly side to side, in a motion not unlike that of a mine detector being carefully passed over a suspected area. As the stork moves its bill, it walks slowly forward, stirring the undergrowth and bottom muck with its feet. When the foot makes cautious contact with a fish, the stork suddenly snaps open its wing on that side, the action and noise often startling the fish into the waiting bill (a delay of only one-fortieth of a second), which clamps shut with the speed (twenty-five milliseconds) and force of a steel trap—one of the most rapid responses known in vertebrates.

This method also enables storks to feed at night, which they sometimes do when there isn't the usual success during the day.

Trying a new feeding place

Fish three inches and under are swallowed immediately; larger ones are killed first by several snaps of the bill, then swallowed. Stork appetites are hearty, one captive stork eating 650 one-inch fish in thirty-five minutes.

The wood storks' simple preference is for lively fish. In tests in captivity, they have eaten dead ones, but only after it was obvious that they would get nothing else to eat. But in the wild they have been observed even discarding live fish that didn't have enough wiggle in them.

Dr. Philip Kahl discovered in an experiment that storks do not rely on sight at all in their unusual touch-and-take technique. To test the tactile reflex, he blackened two halves of a Ping-Pong ball with India ink and glued them over the eyes of a stork, which was then released with another unhandicapped stork in a wading pool full of minnows.

"As they swept their opened bills about," Dr. Kahl observed in *The Living Bird*, "neither seemed to orient visually to the fish, even though the water was clear and the fish were in plain view to the unblinded bird. But whenever a fish swam between the open tips of the bill, the mandibles closed in a flash and the bird came up with a wiggling meal. Blindness seemed no handicap to the one bird. In fact, it caught 19 fish in 40 minutes, more than its companion, which was more easily distracted by my filming the event from nearby."

Dr. Kahl also believes that the striking black-and-white plumage of the wood storks is advantageous for their survival since distant companions can easily spot feeding gatherings from the sky and converge to share the activity.

Another birdman, T. Gilbert Pearson, observed the storks using a different fishing technique. "Before me," he wrote in the National Geographic Society's *The Book of Birds*, "amidst the scattered slender pines and clusters of scrub palmettos, was a shallow pond crowded with wading birds moving rapidly about and making a great commotion. Scratching with their feet, they were muddying the water so that the fish were obliged to rise to the surface to breathe. I had come suddenly upon a flock of wood storks gathering their food in the peculiar, communistic manner they sometimes employ, for when many thus work at the same time they can so pollute the water that their victims quickly appear, to be seized between the birds' large and powerful beaks."

"Scratching with their feet, they were muddying the water ..."

Since most of southern Florida where storks live is less than fifteen feet above sea level and since much of the state's 54,300 square miles is lowland, the region still has sufficient flooded areas where the birds can find food. Fortunately, their fishing territory is varied—freshwater marshes, flag ponds, wet prairies full of dense stands of grasses, the shallow-water parts of cypress heads, and roadside ditches and culvert pools.

Storks are also fortunate in their selection of fishing waters. It has helped secure their survival, for, unlike the brown pelicans that live in the same habitat, the storks use *only* the freshwater and tidal flats that contain the rough fish of little importance to man. Pelicans dive from the sky into the ocean. As a result, they came into competition with commercial fishermen, who declared war and came close to wiping the pelicans out until a law was passed protecting them.

The storks have yet a second bonus: when times get difficult and fish are less abundant in the customary feeding places, the man-made ponds near Corkscrew Swamp Sanctuary can be used until the situation improves.

A final factor enabling our American stork to live out its fourteen-year lifespan is that it does not migrate, and so it does not encounter the hazards that threaten the white stork. But the wood stork does move about in what is called postbreeding dispersal. These small journeys take it to many of the southeastern states during the summer months.

A trio of pelicans skims by.

The American wood stork

Thus, with its unique and relatively secure life style, America's stork could be the subject of the last stork legend. It may become more famous than the fabled species that started all the stories of the stork—by outliving it.